Jervie Hickey

CSU Poetry Series XLI

Other books by Susan Firer:

My Life with the Tsar (New Rivers Press)
The Underground Communion Rail (West End Press)

Susan Firer

The Lives of the Saints
and Everything

Cleveland State University Poetry Center

Acknowledgments

Grateful acknowledgment is made to the following publications, in which some of these poems first appeared.

THE BOUNDARIES OF TWILIGHT: CZECHO-SLOVAK WRITING FROM THE NEW WORLD (New Rivers Press): "Relics"
CHICAGO REVIEW: "Building the House of Crazy," "The Mongolian Contortionist with Pigeons," "Phantom Love"
THE CREAM CITY REVIEW: "I, the Excommunicate," "God Sightings," "The Lives of the Saints," "On the Fairway of Dreams: Nights' Hobos," "Saint Christina the Astonishing, 1224," "Saint Wilgefortis"
DREAMS AND SECRETS, Woodland Pattern Book Center: "My Mother's Garters"
EXIT 13: "Wisconsin. Route 33. Good Friday."
EXQUISITE CORPSE: "Basement Slow Dancing," "The Lessons of Columbus," and "This Is a Thank You Note to That Fat Bouncer God Who Threw Me Out When at Eighteen I Tried to Enter the Suicide House Forever"
IRIS: "The Blue Umbrella Dance"
MOTHERING: "Bay Shore Hosiery"
MS: "My Mothers' Rosaries"
NOSTALGIA: "The Big Blue House"
THE NEXT PARISH OVER: A COLLECTION OF IRISH-AMERICAN WRITING (New Rivers Press): "My Mothers' Rosaries"
SOUTHERN POETRY REVIEW: "The Head-Carriers"

Manufactured in the United States of America

ISBN 1-880834-04-9
    1-880834-05-7 (paper)

Library of Congress Catalog Card Number 93-71915

The Ohio Arts Council helped fund this program with state tax dollars to encourage economic growth, educational excellence and cultural enrichment for all Ohioans.

Contents

for Bix

I

Holy persons draw to themselves all that is earthly.
—*Hildegard of Bingen*

Bay Shore Hosiery

> Clothes have their existence:
> they have colors and patterns
> and forms, and live deep—far
> too deep!—in our myths.
> —*Pablo Neruda*

The store was always long and narrow
like a business envelope. No Radio City
Rockette kicking legs on the walls back then.
Quiet colored stockings came in twos,
like husbands and wives. The years
I'm thinking of I was still
below my mother's waist and
would butt her like a white goat
the whole while the saleswoman queried
colors she might want to see: Cafe
Au Lait? Vanilla Mist?

The boxes on the shelf were thin as
Hershey bars or secrets. I waited for
the moment when the perfumed saleslady would
stick her fist into the sheer color
stocking and spread her fingers like an open fan,
her always Revlon-red-enameled finger-
nailed hand open and spreading
the stocking to show the color
that would be on my mother's leg.

Always, then, every time, I went sloppy
legged weak, cut from animals,
dusted with promise, blown full
of flowers and dreams. I'd become
a city of lights, every part of me
doing the earth's mathematics.
For a moment, I was a succession
of angels, ball lightning, the earth's
geometry fighting levitation.

Then as quickly as it started, the sales
woman would make another fist
and slide it out of the stocking without
making one snag. My mother would be
taking money out of her fragrant black purse
and swiping my cheek with a crumpled purse kleenex
and asking me, if, when we got home,
could she peel my sunburned back, please?

My Mother's Garters

were everywhere, rubber
and metal visitations, key-
holes, scatter pins, always
where you least expected them,
like sleep words, crushed
bees, a country fair you
happen on, wild
asparagus, 4
beautiful albino goldfish.

They branded her thighs,
on each side a sore
red question mark, tropical red.
Often, we couldn't leave the house
until someone found one.

Often other women dug in their fragrant
purses and shared one. They were even
on movie house floors, buses, even
in kitchen drawers. They connected

the seen with the unseen.
They were an excursion over white
skin, cherry orchards in blossom,
a gondola ride in summer, peaches,
magnifying glass shaped.

They left a strange stenography;
it said: Look,
these are only women's bodies
splashing geography,

wet as the world. Touch
one, let it run off on you.

My Mothers' Rosaries

Rosaries of night breath,
rosaries of woman smell,
rosaries of dream, spoon
rosaries blue, rosaries of yarn
knots greed rosaries, dandelion
rosaries, dough rosaries,
crystal Slovac rosaries,
baked potato rosaries, cock
hot rosaries, sunflower
yellow rosaries, phone line
rosaries, human hair
rosaries, butterfly blue
rosaries, snow rosaries,
dark cherry red burn rosaries,
say lead rosaries, flour
white first communion rosaries,
lemon rosaries, cold-cock punch
rosaries, confessional dark
water holy rosaries, sweet apple
red rosaries, concertina sweet rosaries,
before bed rosaries, wild
asparagus rosaries, smooth
wood beaded rosaries, see
all the way to heaven rosaries.
Keep me sighted rosaries,
don't let me be pregnant rosaries,
don't let anyone die rosaries,
bring him here rosaries,
keep me sane rosaries,
keep him off me rosaries.
My mothers' rosaries fill
my mouth with dark prayer names:
My name is Susan the Baptist,

daughter of Ruth Lorraine Brophy
whose mother Katherine Boussart
came from Alsace-Lorraine
with an immigrant's trunk
full of women's lost names,
and prayers, rosaries, Maypoles, and angels.

It Starts to Rain at the Shopping Mall

It starts to pour,
and few of the old, coupon-fisted
ladies at the mall are ready
for it. They all go
to Walgreen's & get plastic shopping
bags & put them on their heads.
The bags look like they're blown
up with helium, they stand 12 inches
straight up from their heads. All
the old women sitting on the plastic
benches, waiting for their rides, look
like white-haired Marge Simpsons.
They turn toward each other, and in
their plastic-bag covered heads they wonder
if there are words in heaven. One
old woman has a plastic rain cap. She unfolds
its clear accordion pleats and puts
it on her Tuesday blue-rinse do and
makes a dash for her car. Her rain bonnet
blows off; it sits in the middle of the patent
leather street, looking just like the word help.

The Acrobats of Death

On the 15th day of my mother's dream morphine,
that said pain was the real dream stuff,
the great trapeze of dead past loves
and family, that she had prayed for earlier,
dropped through the hospital roof.
And my dead father was the catcher, hanging
from his knees above her fireworks of bedsores
body, dressed in cheap blue trapeze tights and
sequins, swinging his arms above her and
whispering, "Ruth, Ruth." She answered, "Why,
Andrew," and grabbed his swinging, muscled arms,
joined the acrobats of death, joined the God
circus. Her skin-bone body loosened
and fell from her, up she came out
from the old skin into a halo
yellow third world circus satin
bare bottom rope trick leotard.
Her cheeks turned evening red,
her fingernails dusty blue,
her hands wax bean yellow. She was a sunset,
a garden, finally in the God circus. Her
laboring breath turned to John Philip
Sousa music. The tubed scarred body
she played tag with death in
turned to light, turned transparent.
Sea urchin pomanders (straight from the ocean
beds in the English Channel), schaum tortes,
English garden sweet peas, black
shoes with gold buckles, pearl earrings
and necklace, a ukulele, bridge cards,
diamonds, and old photographs
fell from her disappearing.
She was my mother in the time
when mothers were like clothes
lines, and the clothes blowing on them were

filled with children. Then she left
with a fragrance complicated as opium,
complicated as parents and children.

Relics

Not fountains, grottoes, or statuary, but pieces
of cloth, bone, wood, and hair touched
to other people or places was what
we found when we undressed you. After
you died, we found a conniption of medals
shinier than the gem collection room in Chicago's
Field Museum. Relics like soldiers' decorations
pinned and blazing on your hospital gown, tulip
green scapulas clamped to the buzzer that called
your nurse. Stuffed in your purse: pieces of uncooked-
spaghetti-colored palm touched to the Holy Cross,
a chip of St. Catherine's bone sealed
& filigreed in metal; a piece of bicycle
blue cloth blessed by the pope & sealed in plastic;
a silver Saint Christopher medal touched
by Padre Pio; a Saint Jude medal.
That late afternoon relics rained deep
as the voice of Bishop Sheen
whose recordings of the rosary you'd played
us to sleep with when we were your baby girls.

The Reliquary of Children

My son sleeps his 5 year old sleep
on prayer hands, like my dead mother
after toast, tomato jam, and buttermilk
used to collapse on her floral couch
at 3 PM for a lurid half hour
of the EDGE OF NIGHT. Delicate
yet as perceptible as a dewclaw,
her presence in the sleeping boy.

Put my thirteen year old daughter's sad
Irish put your foot down & dead bolt eyes,
and my daughter Erin's hands, hands
she will carry through her whole life,
under these assignments of flesh.

Pelted with the bones of sleeping
children and lost desert fathers
and desert mothers whose DNA gifts
come wrapped in children, I remember
my own silent father standing in snow

under frozen clotheslines
in a black leather and fur Russian
(ear and forehead flaps down) hat.
30 below zero and he'd be
throwing suet and seeds to the winter

birds he loved more than anyone
he ever lived with. Like me
he used the eyes of parents
he never knew to not look
at those who loved him.

The Statue Maker

Corposant beauty: tattoos in a velodrome
of breath. Do you dream yourself
older? or younger? In the direction
of light? or the black odd
colors? In our bullseye black nights we all
travel a caravansary of bodies and dreams,
often plumb out of plumb, like litigious
love or a seaside camel ride.

Still tabernacles we all are. As we kiss good
nights, we are people we once dreamt
with breath sweet as lakeside snow. Here I am
a statue maker in a blue sleeping
house. In our ice windowed house I'm the lake
guardian of night cloud cherub and gargoyle;
my hair turns the colors of February
nights' iced windows. I breathe

and touch. Little clearings momentarily open.
I whisper soft as bird shadows:
corn snow this panic of grace
and transubstantiation in our beds
at night, corn snow, corn snow.

The Lives of the Saints

Wildgoose the boy dies over and over in the autumn
leaves. Each Apache death
louder and more disorganized than the previous.
His sister, my daughter, plays Mozart's
"Divertimento No. 2" in our driveway-parked car.
Behind the windshield she looks like a silent
movie star, her mouth forming silent words:
pizzicato, allegretto, arco. Her violin bent
arm and tilted chin no longer look strange
behind the dashboard where she has insisted
on practicing this summer and fall.
"A room of my own," she calls the front seat.
Autumn's boxelder bug black and orange colors, beets'
reds. (Is there any vegetable that tastes more
like the ground it grows in than beets?)
Every season has its own taste and smell:
autumn is extreme unction. The Dairyland Twirlers
practice on the Shorewood high school football
field, their tossed and spinning batons turn to stars,
their tossed and split-legged-costumed bodies
a lovely throw of sequins on twilight. All
early evening under my not yet closed autumn
windows, people hurry walk home through
the confetti, purple-loud leaves. Soon it will be
snow shovel scrape, harps, communion white, and
salters with their orange light topped trucks
spilling blue. But sweet now is this
relic tent of leaves, lighted with all the saints:
Saint Agnes breasts in hand, Saint Antony
ringing bells and riding pigs, my son
and daughter dreaming the wild autumn children
dreams that become their bodies, become the overtures
of their holy, tumultuous, leaf blessed lives.

An Autobiography of an Angel

> The trouble with being a woman, Skeezix,
> is being a little girl in the first place.
>   —*Anne Sexton*

Every May on the Virgin's Holyday,
the whole congregation, in procession, moved
around our Santa Monica Catholic Church. We all
snaked past the football field, down Silver Spring
the business street, past Chicken-Delight, the bank,
the convent, the rectory, the bakery (always the same
wedding cake in the window), back across the
asphalt playground to the statue of the Blessed
Mary where we sang hymns
of love into newly opened spring
windows and wind. And only because I was small
and blond and curly headed, I got to be a flower
crowned angel. I came after the Monsignor, the spring
vestmented priests and altar boys. FORGET THEM!
I got to wear the white satin angel
dress with the beautiful pastel ribbons.
And for one half hour, on an always sunny
May school day afternoon, in new white
patents and pastel-flowered-embroidered undies,
I was a hymn singing angel, carrying a bouquet of God's
flowers in my hands. An angel for a half hour
of procession I was not the child who always broke
windows with hardballs and red rubber suction-tipped
arrows, not the one who threw wet wash cloths
on hot lit light bulbs to hear explosions, not
the child who rifled through her parents' drawers
not knowing what she was looking for. I was
not the child who hid her correction
shoes and bribed the boys for their black hightops,
not the child who, from pretending to be asleep
(keep the eyelids relaxed, the breath even),
knew that Billy's mother was arrested for stealing
bobby pins from Kresge's, knew that the twins' father
had cocktails at lunchtime at Woolf's Island

with a woman who was not the twins' mother.
I was not the one who in winter lay in self-
made elaborately tunneled snow
forts until the whole world was white
except my child body I could float yellow,
not the child who prayed for a horse,
who hated her sister for always being
sick, who chewed red-wax lips and
stuck yellow kernel corn up her nose
until she couldn't breathe and the
fire department had to come to her house.
For twenty minutes of angel time I was
not the girl who wet her pants whenever
she laughed too hard, who hated the smell
of cancer in her Aunt Bea's hospital room,
who hated boys because they could be
altar boys, priests or hobos. For twenty
minutes, I could forget the teenage boy
who had pulled me into my parents' garage
and oddly asked to suck the flat breast
spots on my eight year old body.
For twenty minutes of grade school time,
which for a child I'm sure is like dog years—
7 grade school child hours for every adult's one—
I could forget Mary Margaret, our 8th grade head
cheerleader, who had a brain tumor and had lost
all her beautiful white angel blond angel hair,
could not feed herself, and had to wear diapers.
For twenty minutes I could quit wondering
what the hell was behind Mr. Gunderson's, the
only male teacher in the school, & mine that year,
gray suit's plaid pant's zipper, anyway?
FOR I WAS AN ANGEL,
a May afternoon radium winged flower crowned angel,
deciding, like any other angel, whether to ever
turn back. Like most children I was
a saintly child piñata, filled and waiting
to break over the whole Goddamn village.

In 6th Grade Sister Bernadette Made Us Look Up Our Name Saints in *The Penguin Dictionary of Saints*

Most of the boys were named after apostles: Peter,
Paul, Andrew, John etc. I didn't even know
if there was a Saint Susan. I thought I was named
after a fat aunt from the Old Country, but on p. 316
of Donald Attwaters' *The Penguin*
Dictionary of Modern Saints there it was: Susan,
martyr, beheaded (BEHEADED?) for rejecting the hand
of Diocletian's partner Maximian, "She was the beautiful
niece of the bishop of Rome, Saint Caius," it read. Yeah,
well, I began seeing a common black thread running
through these lives of women saints. The more I read
about them the more I realized
most women saints were BEAUTIFUL,
and, usually, they had rejected the come-
ons of someone more powerful than them.
I stopped washing my hair, started
wearing old boys' black hightops. Nights I prayed
until I glowed like blue-moon ice cream
that I'd never (NEVER) get breasts, which were from all
indicators—movies (CLEOPATRA), magazines, conversations
(She had this pair of knockers etc. etc. bla, bla,
bla . . ."), jokes (which frequently contained ironing
boards or fried eggs), calendars and so on—attractive
to powerful men. J. F .K. was president; Marilyn
Monroe sang happy birthday to him. I prayed
my stomach into Turk's-head knots. My mother made me
"quit the monkeyshines." She made me clean
up for my 6th grade picture. She washed
and rinsed (a rinse of real lemon, set child on
swingset, with lemoned hair, for approximately 10
minutes, hope for a sunny day), and curled (one
big bologna curl around my neck) my hair, pinned
a sprig of cherries on my white lace collar, shot
me behind the ear with a puff of Chanel #5, and

sent me off to the photographer.
He said, "Say cheese." I said, "Saint Susan."

Four weeks later the proofs came in the mail.
My mother beamed: "Look, Honey,
the photographer sent a note with them." The note
read: Tell this girl she is BEAUTIFUL.
She should be a model. I saw my head on a platter,
it was on a yo-yo string, it was
in Ed Gein's living room. Mrs. Wolff
was right again: "Suffer for beauty," she told us
all too many times, and I thought I was finally
beginning to get her drift. I thought of the saints'
mortified lives, visions, miracles and other
remarkable occurrences. I thought of Mary Margaret Fagan
walking home after school night
after night struggling to stay upright
under the weight of her black-cased tuba.

The Lessons of Columbus

Sister Arleen drew four straight lines IIII ,
when she drew a line diagonally through those four
(JHT) you got a pagan baby. On the board
pagan babies looked like the turtle totem (🐢)
Chingachgook had tattooed on his chest in *The Last
of the Mohicans*. The nuns
chalked up pagan babies like movie prisoners
counted days on their cells' walls.
Pagan babies cost $5 each. Sister Arleen drew
white chalk pagan baby outlines on the green
blackboard to remind us of our job. OUR JOB,
clearly set forth to us each morning after Mass
while we ate our cold, paper-sack breakfasts,
was to save enough money to buy the most pagan
babies possible (sort of a C.A.R.E. program
for baby souls). I pictured the babies
wearing turbans, jeweled and pierced bodies,
(maybe baby sword swallowers)
colored like sea beans or pumpkins, sleeping
in baby hammocks tied between palm trees
in smoky villages, living under palm fronds.
Buoyed by potential grace, I begged to polish
my mother's silver, wash windows, dust.
In each polished surface I saw another smiling pagan
baby's face. I was Saint Teresa, Saint Agnes,
one of the girls from Fatima, I was Saint Susan,
skipping the Fox Bay Movie Theatre sparkle
sidewalks and aiming for !!PAGAN BABIES!!

And I did it, on my very own, I
earned, and saved, and bought, 10
(JHT JHT JHT JHT JHT JHT JHT JHT JHT JHT)
pagan babies (🐢🐢🐢🐢🐢🐢🐢🐢🐢🐢). That year
I was 10, I was ironed by Scott Sauer,
who until the very last day of pagan babies

did not have one, not one, line behind his name.
That last morning of pagan babies he breezed
in late (DID NOT make it to Mass), threw $100
($100) on Sister Arleen's always neat desk,
and went back to his own where he folded himself
in for the day. Scott Sauer, the worst boy in class
(he smoked, snapped older girls' bras, and had already
made out), had bought 20 (twenty) PAGAN BABIES:
🜨🜨🜨🜨🜨🜨🜨🜨 🜨🜨🜨🜨🜨🜨 🜨🜨🜨🜨🜨🜨.
(Scott's Dad owned the local Cadillac dealership;
he always made sure each nun had her own television
during the World Series, which nuns put right up there
with Christmas.) That day still reads
like a math problem to me: At $5 a pagan baby,
Scott, doing nothing on his own, has saved
twenty pagan babies. At the same price, Susan,
working illegally hard for a month, has saved
ten pagan babies—who has more grace? Scott?
or Susan? How much does each one have? Reduce
to a common denominator (who cares?)
and show your process. I couldn't figure it. So,
as I often did in those days, I asked myself, what
would Christopher Columbus do if he were
in my shoes? I knocked back, straightened
my new, white, go-go boots and continued on
the always emigration from self, sailing
star acid lost on DNA & its trailing comet grace.

Basement Slow Dancing

> Fear walks the world of the words
> which pertain to our bodies.
> —*Pablo Neruda*

I have forgotten whose basement it was,
but I remember blue electric
waterfall beer signs and an olive
green-musty sofa, and crepe-paper,
a 60's big-haired girl group on
the record player, and we were 13 & slow
dancing. (13, the best age to
slow dance: hardly anything precedes
the dance; certainly, nothing follows it.
It's all dance, an introduction
to the always from then on
mystery of the opposite.) We all were
like a field of yellow globe flowers
that always seem about to open,
but never do. All of us swayed
together in the basement dark,
in the night dark, in the dark
of our coming bodies and lives.
I didn't know what it was that
first time; I didn't even have a name
for it (that would come later
through jokes filled with pencils
and pockets). The important fact
is that all the words people taught me:
erection, hammer, hot rod, pole, hard-on,
boner, rock candy—all the words were wrong,
were too callous, too flippant, too steely
for that sweet nudging, that strange
insistent champagne christening ghost
floating into me and finding a ghost partner
voyager who walked out of me to meet it.
This was not movie love fireworks or waves.
This was older: pumpkins falling in on themselves,

black fields shooting up purple, yellow, and pink
colors on dark, fragrant nights. This was kissing
your parents' dead, white bones then eating
from them. How many things are
our bodies too dumb to name, but smart enough
to remember? Our bodies were dancing
in dark beer sign lit basements to music
that only our bodies understood. Our bodies
were clinging to each other, helping each
other grow toward where we all would.
Like spoons that fit the mouth so perfectly
you never want to take them out, we were
dancing, perfectly, feeding the bodies forever
forecasts of one and another.

In This House of Skin

All the times we have joined our bodies
float us in some ghosty placenta that seals
us from the always scream siren of God.
All our times of love follow us: the white
haired mother whose hair we combed
on her death bed, the children
who have lived in our skin bodies,
the children who have died in our skin
bodies, the bodies we have lived in,
our sweet cemetery bodies,
others' sweet cemetery bodies,
the men we have refused to touch,
the men we have touched,
the first boy we slow danced with who got a hard-on,
the girls we've fed bird songs to,
everyone we've ever dream made love to,
in our bodies' long conga lines of love
our hips smile shake off all their scars,
love's always free lunch feeding us
its always wild sweet dark. We collect
the memory photos of love's foreign travels:
the railroad man in Alaska,
the bull fighter in California,
the pregnant Indian woman under a world-
map umbrella, the children with bruised blue
summer lake swimming lips, the women of our
childhood who wore fur-trimmed, ankle snow boots,
Aunt Virge conga-ing with Diamond Jim,
under the cottonwoods, Sister
Theresine walking a black ghost into her Christ
wedding. Our times of love tie us to earth
with sunflowers, with blue yarn, anemones
rustling in our palms, bougainvillea in our veins.
Each moment of love is a deferred payment
on death. Have you ever felt

it all fall on you? All the congas of bodies
past, quivering with psalms, glittering
with stains, chainsaw hearts packed away?
I'm telling you about the yo-yo magic of love
that wasp stings, that moves us all like red checkers.
In the trade winds of love's breathing hearts, I call
to all of your applesauce hearts: here, I'll start:
Will you come to me like a bullet?
A tumbleweed?
Or a Mother Mary blue colored blanket?

The Suicide Sister's Dance Hall Heart
Visits the Romance Factory

On weekends people dress in snow-
mobile suits and ride snow-
mobiles to Polynesian restaurants
where miniature paper umbrellas are
the elegance that keeps
them warm on their 40-below-
drunk-wind-chill, bar-stopping
snow-mobile rides home.
(Fact: Everyone is overweight.)

The men love each other
more than the women they will spend
their lives with. The men do things
together: kill
deer and drive around
with their bullet-polka-dotted
dead bodies tied to their
car roofs. The deers' tongues
fall from their mouths slap
against the cars' windows.

Together the guys fish and nail
the fish heads to their garages.
They love cards: poker & sheepshead,
and motors, and guns. At night
they throw bar dice, throw bones. Sometimes,
just for the fun of it, the bartender
has a little, crotchless, black, Frederick's
number behind the bar for the winner,
for the fun of it. The winner will

take it home, wake his sleeping wife
and throw the thing at her. He will be
passed out before she discovers

what it is, that she is too fat
for it, that he is already passed out,
that her crying is louder
than his sleep apnea.

Their beautiful translucent children
shave their heads or grow jungle
beautiful wild hair, or shave half
of their heads & grow the rest.
They pierce their noses, pierce their
ears, pierce their tongues, pierce
their nipples, pierce their sexes.
They scald themselves, drink to toxicity,
drive their cars into trees.
They shoot themselves in the divine
search for a tender connection. While
all around us all the world
with its effortless beauty keeps
giving up potatoes & moonlight & birds.

This Big Blue House

When we bought this blue
house, before the mudjacks
laid the sidewalk, I
carefully placed in the ground,
that the cement would cover,
a small berry-red ceramic heart &
a half-dollar size wooden kiss.

It has snowed on them, of course
rained. Rainbows have scumbled
the cement. Children have parachuted
there, and soft animals have rested.
The neighborhood children have traced
& colored their loud silhouettes, and
tongue sized warblers have dropped

songs like wet yellow paint
here. When my father was cold
in his casket, hands handcuffed
with rosary beads, I slipped the love
poem we always in life kept from each
other into his gray-death-suit-hip-
pocket. I have also buried my mother,

a child that fell from me, an older
sister, sometimes hope, sometimes joy.
But, then, always,
from the wheelchair of my heart
comes the magic act of the bouquets
we've been, what we'll be, what we've
buried and what we will bury and
walk over and toward. When

you come to my blue house, you walk
over all this, and more. What is
the last song you'll sing in your life?
What have you buried that you return to?
Do you really think it's skin
that holds your life together?

The Gray Shape of Wasps' Nests

At the river house there were cherries
on trees that filled with birds and black
nights, cherries on window curtains, on bed
coverings, in bunches on ladies' white
embroidered collars, tied into little girls'
pony tails: cherries ripe and spilling darkness.

Those years fireflies outlined us as night
outlined the magic we all were. I
tamed blue jays to ride my shoulder
and drink from milk blue bowls. In autumn
there were always tomato windowsills
bags of ripening tomatoes and newspaper
wrapped pears and red potatoes.

In the Mississippi flyway in autumn,
we lived under a ceiling of Canada
geese. The feathers fell so
slowly gray as wasps' nests.
Winters were long
skates up the river's wind
shaped ice to the pavilion.

The winter we moved, my father
promised he would drive me back in spring,
let me sit in a tree of cherry blossoms
"if only you'll stop all that crying."
The new house had a four arched entrance.
There were arches everywhere.

Three arches that got consecutively smaller ran
up the staircase. At Christmas each child
was placed in an arch & the Christmas photo snapped.
That was a house filled with frames,
and everyone started wiggling or actually
falling out of their own portrait.

Hand painted enamel pulls on every drawer,
and great ceramic fruit baskets on butler tables.
I missed the cherries. In that new house,
there were silver martini shakers and glasses.
I am telling you about the mother country:
long drives to the fox country for lunch,
hot chocolate at the Women's Exchange,
bridge tallies, bathing suits you couldn't get wet.
Always the river getting farther away.

Nights, I'd dream my two sisters and me,
bear cubs on pastel colored ribbon leashes,
wreathes of bells harnessed around us ringing
as we were walked in step together.
My father surrounded by elegant
dark cherry wood furniture knelt
each night beside his poster bed. Sometimes

going to the bathroom, I'd see him
in his dark room, his head resting
on one hand, his elbow on the white
bedspread, his knees in the dark
roses swirling on the floor.
It was in that arched house his hands started flying
wildly in his sleep. Every morning there were new

nicks and gashes his wedding band cut
into the headboard of the dark cherry wood
poster bed. Depending on how you looked,
they always looked different: distant birds,
pieces of maps, bits of stars, or awful little smiles.

Just Past the Slovene Motel and Next to the Holiday Inn in Eveleth, Minnesota Is the Hockey Hall of Fame

The entrance is behind the 25 foot steel hockey stick.

After you pay, run past the jerseys from every team display,
and skip the state tournament videos on TV's everywhere,
forget "The Protective Equipment Used In Hockey Today" display.

If you have to, take a quick trip
through THE ORIGIN
AND EVOLUTION OF HOCKEY TUNNEL;
it's OK. It reads like this:

HOCKEY LIKE GAMES OF THE PAST
(Here look at the photo of the fresco of nude
Greeks playing with sticks and balls.)

OLD GAMES OF SHINNEY AND BRANDY,
including Brandy rules in England around 1850.

"How or where the first puck came to be
no one knows . . . but some historians surmise
it was inevitable
as players tired of chasing a round
bouncing ball over surrounding fields."

"It has been claimed that the earliest hockey
played was by the Imperial Army at Halifax
sometime before 1855."

You get the idea. Move on fast.
Only give a glance from the balcony
to the HOCKEY HALL OF FAMERS:
Hobey Baker, Ike Ikola etc.

You're getting close. It's right
across from the EVOLUTION

OF THE STICK & PUCK wall: A whole shimmering
glass wall of skates.
(Go late fall, possibly late October,
like we did, and no one else will be
there.) Stand in front of the glass,
look at the skates,
read their names: Rocker Skates,
Strap & Clamp Skates,
Nova Scotia Rocker Skates (1850), Old
English Shell Skates (1890) with Brass Tops,
Folding Skates, Aluminum Top Peck & Snyder Skates,
Clamp Hockey Skates, Flanged Skates,
Key Clamp Skates, Brownie Crucible Steel Rocker
Skates, Immigrant Wood Topped Skates With Turned Up
Runners (Brought From Holland), Barney & Berry
Safety Edge Hockey Skate Of 1898,
Union Hardware Cast Steel Hockey Skates (1905),
Barney & Berry Figure Skating High Heel Shoe Skates,
Nester Johnson Factory Assembled Speed
Shoe Skates, and Old Chicago Rollerskates
Of 1880 With Cast Iron Supports,
Steel Top Fastened On With Straps & Key Clamp,
Fiber 3-Piece Pegged Together Wheels.

These skate names are the lost libretto
for Sibelius' FINLANDIA, they are
the ice-cracking composition of Thoreau's
winter pond, they are the sound
of being dead and buried in diamonds &
children's hands are playing in your bone
and diamond grave as if you were a sandbox.

How to calm down after this?
I found the museum's miniature hockey rink:
boards, sticks, pucks.
"Put your shirt back on," my husband yelled
after my sixth goal,
"They probably have surveillance cameras."

If you're alone, you could calm down
at the WM Thayer Tuit Medal Collection.
Do the names:
      Key To The City Of Prague Mantra
      Helsinki World Medal Mantra
Whatever works.

I nearly skipped the place, nearly
took a raincheck. I'll tell you one thing:
It made me reconsider my stance on
THE GREYHOUND ORIGIN DISPLAY MUSEUM
with its "pictorial displays, artifacts, and
Greyhound memorabilia." I tossed
my Eveleth, Minnesota 12 inch miniature
hockey stick souvenir over my shoulder
& made the twenty minute trip
up the road to Hibbing:
HOME OF BOB DYLAN,
HOME OF THE FIRST GREYHOUND.

The Blue Umbrella Dance

I
On this Fat Tuesday, umbrellas
are carrying the people of Milwaukee
like gondolas. I realize I am all
blue today even my brown leather
boots turn blue as Easter
as they dip into puddles. Everyone
looks lovely under an umbrella, no matter
what they are carrying in their pockets.
What makes us want
to put our legs around horses?
Kiss strangers under umbrellas?
Eat mollusks? Care about trilobites?

II
Look, over there, that lady is carrying
a swarm of bees on a crowbar. And next to her
a man yawns under a watermelon frown.
A peacock shivers its eyed tail into erection
in this garden of bright. In this thick
lake smelt smelling fog let me take you
to the fragrant douglas fir. We can
make love under its blowing, bowing arms;
it carries the same sweet amnesty
and honesty of umbrellas and birds' nests.
A little boy is carrying his sister's umbrella;
he is breathing under antlers of umbrellas.

III
I think people take on the decorative holiness
of grottoes under umbrellas: stalactites, picnics,
geodes, love-ins, the Holy Family,
Saint Barbara. All over umbrellas
are popping up like kangaroos, coral reefs,
pistols and amusement parks. I smell
popcorn, do you?

IV
From under an amber and blue world
decorated umbrella a startled "ouch."
(Someone's finger has been pinched
in their own umbrella's mechanism.)
And I mumbling about beauty & pain &
love rush over to kiss the slightly
swelling finger. Watch how
in the tunnels of careworn
umbrella softened lights
how easily the fortresses of rain
and love completely collapse.

On the Fairway of Dreams: Nights' Hobos

I wake in night's plum dark. The small
boy, his pillow over his shoulder
comes to me. He is covered in night.
Later when I get up in the still
dark morning, the boy turns
over into the heat I rise from,
his mouth full of crushed words
bright as fall bees, bright as
trick lips. In my first waking,
I still keep my own dream
where my father's words are
punctuated with shiny apple seeds.
My arms hallucinate my dead
mother; she smells of mint,
black morning fry pans, chrysanthemums.
(This summer I fell in love with the arc
and arch of sprinklers, twilight sprinklers,
afternoon smashed with children & sun
spinning sprinklers, water hallucinations
of arm & heart sprinklers, elevator numbers,
phone booths & boat house sprinklers.)
My father always sat in a dark room.
Sometimes I still hear his breathing.
I am the chemistry of loss and now in this halo
exhilarated exile of body. My husband
has fallen in love with the light of night
tennis courts, not the game, the bright
cellophane falling light. I call
to him in the blackberry purple empty
house. Gem stones fall.
I kimono kiss the windows.
In the swamp dark ruckus of all houses
of desire there are hand job dreams &
storm doors, iron ranges (Mesabi)
and sycamores, detour signs & dollar signs,

Venezuelan silver stars,
and other refuges & magic lullabies.
Once I started wanting, I could not stop.
Look at my musky-mouthed hands.
Look at my night. I am all
these people we married together. I am
beautifully tarred and feathered with all
nights' hobos and Gods.

Wisconsin. Route 33. Good Friday.

Out of the dream of maps and yellow
whipping forsythia, we drive west past
black & purple material-draped twelve
foot wooden crosses. We drive the gray map line
named 33. From Lake Michigan to the Mississippi
River, geese shadows all over the road. In the Coulee
Region we are eccentric in our midnight blue
car. We stop for cokes at THE FOUR WINOS MOTEL
(actually THE FOUR WINDS MOTEL, but the grass
green neon D looks like an O). My husband's
happy here amongst the NIGHT CRAWLERS FOR SALE
signs in every yard. Our three-year-old has peed
in his pants; they are flying like a fat boy
from our car's antenna. Since my talk on personal
spontaneous combustion, our daughters in the back
seat are quiet. And we're all full of the Baraboo
Bakery's blueberry turnovers, Easter cutouts &
sauerkraut rye. In our car grotto we are
eccentric as yeast, as hydrangea, as tilefish.
We are out looking under white marble stars
for the shugging white holy places. At midnight,
we drive past a 20-foot-long, jockey-brief-clad Jim
Palmer blessing us on our Wisconsin journeys.
Our children breathe songs & sleep. We all
are disappearing, always disappearing
into cross-peppered cornfields.

II

I believe in anything.
—*Mary Oliver*

Phantom Love

Pablo Neruda, what were you doing with
a lap full of orange peels, sitting
in the rust colored stratolounger
that someone, during night, put
into Lake Michigan? You reclining
head back, feet up, catching the white
waves splashing like spaetzels
all around you. I
could hear you reciting "Elephant":
>   "Gross innocent
>   Saint Elephant
>   blessed beast . . ."

Why a visitation here in the land of Mars
Cheesecastles, knockwurst, headcheese,
sheepshead, Esterhazy Schnitzel,
Great Lakes Dragaway and steak Tartar?
Your eyes smiled daises when the heavy lady
walking by you looked savagely at her husband
and said: "To hell with deviled eggs."

Pablo, do you, like me, believe
everywhere is beautiful,
and we should try to visit all places
or maybe stay in one place long
enough to know everywhere and one
through it until one is transparent
with butterflies waiting to start
their holy migration to everywhere?

How beneficently you accepted the Moosehead beer
I offered you. I loved our beach volleyball game.
Did you come to me because I used your line on clothes
as an epigraph on the poem I wrote about my mother's
hosiery? Did you come to me to relieve my terrors?

Because we both love Anne Sexton & artichokes?
(Does Anne Sexton read her poems in heaven?)

Did you come to me because we share a belief
in an impure poetry, one soiled and stained
with our "shameful behavior . . .
vigils and dreams . . . declarations
of loathing, love . . . and beasts"?

I took you to the Santa Monica convent to see three
nuns' coats on the convent's clothesline,
each coat blown full and black with God.
On the evening news we
watched together the story of a baby
who that morning had fallen
through a third floor window screen
down three stories to bushes
that caught and held the child unharmed
until her panicked parents reached her.
You told me Lorca's holy dismembered hands
were in the bushes and instantly
I knew it true. Phantom hands.

Under the night's sky cat's cradle of electrical
lines, pink balloon clouds, sprinklers & candles,
we talked of things falling apart
and the beauty as they do,
and after they do,
and before they do.
We decided to go to a concertina bar.
On the way there, I told you about the baseball
pitcher and the pain
he still feels in his amputated arm.
His arm floats in heaven; still it burns
with phantom pain, and I recognize
this phantom pain as the doppelganger
of the phantom love I carry for all
who are a part of me but gone.

Pablo, Pablo, Pablo,
you left the concertina bar so early,
and I knew not to follow you.
Two peppermint schnapps later, again alone, I left
the bar the single hero of my own
night. I noticed
a spring storm had emptied the trees
of blossoms and littered the patent leather
streets, and ground, and parked cars.
I came to my own blossom covered car,
turned on the car lights, the car wipers:
blossom storm. I drove off in
what looked like some great prehistoric
blossom animal, and I, filled
with concertina music, poems and butterflies,
migrated in the always
flyway of fragrant blossoms and phantom loves.

Building the House of Crazy

Children's brass knuckles,
the wild God grace of hills,
a stupor of saints,
a cardboard box of snow.
The world often
too hot to touch, shimmering
with cosmic astonishment & palomino
songs. A butterbean bald baby,
the fidgety incense of childhood,
the smell of burning angels.
A woman, me, knocked down in daylight,
for moments a Christmas red punching bag
hung from basement rafters, hit &
slapped by an ugly stink with brown teeth
who smiles & grabs his cock saying,
"How'dja like a mess of this?"
Midnight lake birds fly soap white
in the city's freeway
billboard kleig light showers.
Summer, the season of love & prayer.
Can you float your prayers into the great
nothing, that so often gives us back that:
nothing. Dancing Christmas in saints, I
ask you, did you ever want
to be anything? Knowing
the warped touches of love & God
& the ravines of crazy in our civilizing
cities, I ask you, who will last
touch your certain dead body? Who
will you last touch? Under
summer festival's blue striped tents,
old women Slovene polka together
to the "Blue Skirt Waltz" & I,
on streets with saints' names
(Blvd. St. Michel, St. Paul),

rummage toward their unstrung light,
charting my body's ruptured bilocations.
Backstage of myself, I'm defining beauty,
barefoot in the whisper slipper of saints'
songs. He saw me bruised with hours, a scar,
a whiteout guest of violence,
a certain yellow outline meant for cement.

This Is a Thank You to That Fat Bouncer God Who Threw Me Out When at Eighteen I Tried To Enter the Suicide House Forever

I remember I was tired, especially
of the married men who wouldn't leave
my new body, that I didn't even know
yet, alone.

I was tired of running from the great
marriage lockup that was sewn into
my future by sex since birth.
I was tired

of bar boys hung like horses
with leather and studs and not
a truth in one
of their tattooed bodies.

I was tired of the inescapable
terribleness of gender
that stretched swelling dreams like flapping
circus tents around me.

One winter night, when I was 15,
I came home to a house of cherry-topped
ambulances and doctors. My mother
slapped two 20's into my hand.

"Take a friend to dinner,"
She said. When I came home,
they were all still
there. Dr. De Groat was trying

to talk my mother into committing
my sister, who like a strobe light, was
wildly hallucinating in the dark
room where they had put her after

they caught her in her baby blue,
baby doll p.j.'s, ringing the neighbors'
suburban door bells, putting a page of Proust
and a page of *Madame Bovary*, in French, in

each answering hand. My 17-year-old sister
yelled my name from the dark room:
"Susan, Susan," her pill-overdosed voice
and call were frightening as money.

My mother wouldn't sign. My sister
came part way back. Three years later
I was eighteen when I crossed
my hands in the death-appropriate way

and knocked on God's door. She
threw me out in a black night of puking.
My ears rang Her church bells for a year.
My eyes looked Xed out like funny-paper people.

Still, I want to thank God for recognizing I
was still on training wheels. I
want to thank God for carding me,
saying "You're too young to enter."

I want to thank Her for returning
me, all my bits of stupid floating
yellow as confetti, as polka
dots around me, for dropping

me back into my body's skin machinery
like a 20 below winter-chilled
bird falling from a warm
chimney to sidewalk ice.

I came back tulip boned and weakened
to ponds of stone hearts. A bag of flesh
born on From Me To You Street,
a jink and I was back,

holy and tattered, beautiful
and scarred full of prayer,
empty of pills, wide-hearted
with wonder.

And now, years later, I want to thank Her for all
the dusty blue mornings since on planet rodeo
with all their rain thumps and knocks,
all the yellow as school bus autumns,
and magic as snow springs, for paper-
boys & papergirls, the spangle of mum-mum moons,
artichokes and Alaska,
the holy hard-ons of sweet
men, and for the beautiful crystal
planetarium of children, and for the kiss
and tuck of Professor Longhair and
Old Crow on wind bucking nights.

I want to thank the dark, liquid suck of God
for the Church Of The Holy Innocents
on Waldo Blvd. in Manitowoc, Wisconsin
with its twenty-foot-tall electric rosary

lit in the woods next to the church at night,
the electric rosary a lasso, an invitation
anyone can walk through, a gift, better than appliances
that last longer than the marriages that purchase them.

Oh, spaghetti hearts, even if just for once,
listen to me. Do not hot rush death;
stop at maypoles, bird cages, & scuppernong
marshes and marl. Anyways, always,
we are turning into weather & boulders
while the world spins teal beautiful
around us while we take our great short around God detours.

Of This See

Bareback under the maiming stars,
on our avant-garde planet, all
these vaults of sanctity and me,
this nervous idea, this dance
hall heart & her sad blundering medicine
show making its way, toward you
through all the exaggerations of blood
across our canasta planet, across our pop-
rock planet, across the suicide
impatience of now, past winter
branches topped with lost mittens waving
royal blue & wine machine-knit good-byes
and hi's, I stomp on our sweet
pimento saint-stuffed planet,
and all the early winter night windows
buckle with their yellow light, let go
of their visions: in the beauty
parlor window I walk past,
a woman sits in the yellow night beauty
parlor windows, wrapped in a black slick
tent to collect her falling hair relics.
Another standing woman holds a scissors
at the back of her neck. A miniature
white poodle with a red bow looks stapled
on the sitting women's black tented lap.
The surrounding snow freezes in the most
amazing light. A silent gold painted
harp is framed in a window on Downer.
Through this magenta, magnetic pot shot
storm of saints, I travel with children
who write on bricks: "There is a light
that never goes out." I take the photos
as they bend and kiss of who & why they love.

Saint John, not the John
whose head Salome asked Herod for

for her charm bracelet, but John
the author of the fourth Gospel,
3 biblical epistles,
and the book of Revelation,
St. John the Apostle,
the evangelist,
a.k.a. "The Divine" (this before John Waters),
John, brother of St. James the Greater,
son of Zebedee,
1/2 of the 2 known as the "Sons of Thunder,"
impetuous St. John one of the pillars of the church,
when he was so old it was difficult to talk
would simply say to assembled crowds:
"Love one another,
that is the Lord's command;
and if you keep it,
that by itself is enough."

And to help us we have solitariness, weeping icons,
sleepless monks, & Taco Bell, the desert fathers &
mothers, visitations & curing waters, cappuccino,
blood relics & snow, flowering aprons, levitations,
leper houses, soft beautiful animals, butterfly-
winged angels, hermits, carrots, mountains,
& scallops & sunflowers & the stories of saints
with their robber councils, tortures, visions,
beheadings, vindications, romances, weddings &
revelations, ecstasies & bilocations, healings &
prophecies & predators & monasteries & in the stories
of the saints are our own stories.

saint (sānt) *n.* 1. *Abbr.* S., St.
Theology a. A person officially recognized
by the Roman Catholic church and certain
other Christian churches as being entitled
to public veneration and as being capable
of interceding for women on earth;

one who has been canonized.
b. Any person who has died
    and gone to heaven.
c. Any baptized believer in Christ,
    according to the New Testament.
2. A very holy person.
3. A charitable, unselfish, or
    patient person.

"Do not fear:
no harm can touch
your souls whatever
infamy is inflicted
on your bodies,"
said Eulogius to Flora & Mary
who the African Moslem ruler
Abd ar-Rahman II was threatening
with prostitution unless they apostatized.

And I have painted DO NOT FEAR
in pistachio red letters on the stone
colored medicine show that rolls slide
trombone bright toward you
on the spinning, sparking wheel bodies
of saints who hold their feet & hands
in the sturdy wheel shape of salvation.

The Head-Carriers

St. Dionysius was claimed as a cephalophore or
head-carrier: that is, one of the martyrs who was
said to have carried his severed head to his place of
burial.

These are the always Halloween: Trick-
or-Treat, these are the beheaded,
who carry their skins like just picked up
dry cleaning, or wine red fall wraps
over their arms, those who ghost
walk towards their lost heads or sex
(or maybe like St. Cadoc, whose main form
of transportation was a cloud, maybe
they cloud ride to find their lost parts),
singing: ALL E ALL E OTTS IN FREE OOO.
I have seen them, these saints with knives
between their legs because of their sex,
with bullets rattling in their pure
skulls because of their skin pigment.
These are the poor who live on the wrong
streets, wear a leather jacket, are
the out of power sex, who are shot
in their dream lovely sleep beds. I
have seen them carrying their blue faces
towards their bodies, like tasteful navy
wrist bags, or like red netted bags of fall
onions. I have seen Saint Agnes carrying
her cut off breasts on a platter,
like black tulip bulbs wanting only dark
and earth and their own buried ribboned
bodies. These are the saints of Burleigh
Street and Center Street, 19th & Walnut
& every other street and sex you'd be
afraid to walk on or in, leaving yellow
outlines of their martyred bodies,
yellow halos, reminding us of the always
sweet luggage of skin and fear, holding us

together, separating us from the always
waiting white flowers, from Saint David's
singing doves, St. Columban's bears,
St. Bernard's beehives & St. Cajetan's
benevolent pawnshops.

Genesius The Actor

Lope de Vega, Jean de Rotrou, Karl Löwe, Felix
Weingartner, and Henri Ghéon, all have acted
or sung the drama of Genesius the Actor.
While entertaining Diocletian in a scream skit,
mocking Christian baptism, the grace of God
touched Genesius, like a bit of bad
electrical work: a foot in the tub,
a hand around the curling
iron. When presented to Diocletian
after the performance, Genesius spilled
the beans, talked turkey, explained
he'd been converted to Christ, during
the performance. Immediately he was put
to torture. When he wouldn't give
in, you guessed it: another cephalophore.
Look I can go with this. Just because
the same story is told about 3 other actor
martyrs (Ardalio, Gilasius of Heliopolis,
& Porphyry) doesn't queer it for me. I
just wish grace didn't so very often come down
like a car crash with ghost people trying to unite
their bruised-blueberry-blue-heads
with their torn & scatter-tortured bodies.
I wish grace could be as beautiful as the language
of drugs: heroin's green balloon, cocaine's angel
dust. I wish grace could be that beautiful
with none of the reality crash torture down to it.

Saint Wilgefortis

Like most women saints, she
preferred to be a virgin, "Consecrated
her maidenhood to God," one
big lollipop of love. Her father,
the king of Portugal, had other ideas:
"Darling, you will marry my friend,
the king of Sicily." (What a deal.)
Saint Wilgefortis turned to God.
She prayed white to God, prayed
James Brown loud, Wilson
Pickett sincere until God sent her
a big, black-hairy beard. Beard
happy, she'd run it through the tunnel
of her hand like a magician's silk
scarf trick. She'd shake crumbs
from it after meals. When
the king of Sicily saw her, he
nearly lost his cookies.
Her father had her crucified pronto,
on the spot, one big
bearded X on a cross. She
is the bearded woman on the cross.
(Some people say she looks a lot like
Christ.) In England, she is a.k.a.
Saint Uncumber; English women,
having nowhere else to turn to,
still sneak prayers to her, like 1920's
American women snuck cigarettes, like
contemporary women sneak food. In the loo,
in their gardens, the English women still
knee drop to prayer,
giving Uncumber the whole rotten story
of their troublesome husbands
(who run over them like tar trucks),
and their families, and their
own bearded faces and lives.

An Amateur's Guide to Invocations, Emblems, Patrons, Patronesses, & Prayer

> How I pray is breathe.
> —*Thomas Merton*

A Saint Nervous Breakdown

More impressive than Ripley's Believe It Or Not
Museum these saints' stories are. Saint Bartholomew's
emblem is a butcher knife, St. Julian the Hospitaller
is the patron saint of circus people. Come to this
Nautilus machine of saints' spirits, these strange
noodles, accessible as K-Mart, this fix of saints.
St. Francis of Sales is the patron saint of writers.
"Religious devotion," Sales wrote, "does not destroy:
it perfects; it is a mistake, a heresy, to want
to exclude devoutness of life from among soldiers,
from shops, and offices, from royal courts.
from the homes of the married."
In case of toothache, invoke St. Apollonia.

St. Fiacre, who was very strict
in excluding women from his own
enclosure—stories are still told
about the misfortunes he brought down
on trespassing women, which makes me
wonder what he would have done with the always
trespassing Grace Paley who climbs America's
nuclear fences & other barriers—
St. Fiacre is invoked especially by persons
suffering from "haemorroids." My
Penguin Saints doesn't say why,
or if it is okay for "haemorroid" suffering
women to invoke him. (My inclination
would be not to.) Anyway, Fiacre's emblem
in art is the spade, because he's the patron
saint of gardeners, because of the fine vegetables
he grew around his hermitage in Paris.

Pope Sixtus V, looking at a picture of St. Jerome
beating his breast with a stone said,
"You do well thus to use that stone: without it
you would never have been numbered among the saints."
Mother Cabrini, patroness of all emigrants,
could be the patroness of surprise. She
wanted to go to China but ended up in Chicago.
(That cowboy hearted Leo XIII said: "Do not
go to the East, but to the West.") Mother
Cabrini became the first citizen of the U.S.
to be canonized as a saint. Surprise. Confetti
Chicago hot dogs. You, come immigrate

to these fields lit ticker tape with saints. Walk.
(The average person walks the equivalent of 4-1/2 trips
around the planet in a lifetime.) Who would you
rather walk with—St. Malachy who it was said of
"His first and greatest miracle was himself . . .
there was nothing in his behavior that could offend
anyone"—or would you like to mosh with Christina
the Astonishing who offended everyone. She behaved
"in a terrifying manner." Sweet, wild, river-jumping
Christina, who was often chained up for her own safety.
(One priest broke her leg to slow her down.)
Who will help you decide? Who will help you
interior decorate your custody of skin & soul?
St. Dympna patroness of the insane?
St. Dunstan's emblem is a pair of tongs.
Edward the Confessor's emblem is a finger ring.
St. Hyacinth of Cracow, the wonderworker,
has the most mysterious blue-flower name.

A Diet of Saints

Genevieve, patroness of Paris, stayed
"an epidemic of ergot-poisoning, 'burning
sickness,' " when her relics were carried
in public procession. (Who thought of this?

We're all sick: let's carry Genevieve's
bones around Paris, so we'll feel better.)
No pink Pepto Bismol yet, so they punted.
It worked. Still, annually, in Paris churches,
Genevieve's butter-pecan-colored bones
are hoisted, & ergot-poisoning is zilch—
a thing of the past. Whose bones should we hoist?
St. Agatha's emblem is 2 breasts on a dish.
St. George is patron saint of the kingdom
of England, and of boy-scouts. His deeds
we're told "are known only to God."
Although there is a lot of gossip
about his dragon killing. *The Penguin
Dictionary of Saints* says: "No
historical particulars of his life have survived;
such are the vagaries of his legend
that earnest endeavors have been made to prove
that he never existed, or
that he was somebody else."

A Weather of Saints: a Panhandle Hook of Saints

St. Dominic's emblems are a star
& a dog with a torch in his mouth.
(He's the saint the singing nun Dominiqued about:
"Dominique-inique-inique. . . ."
The singing nun wasn't happy. After the Ed Sullivan
(really bigg) show, she went back to Belgium
& cold quit the convent. She ended
up doing the suicide thing with her lady lover.
The best thing Belgium ever gave her is her grave,
gaudy as Elvis in Las Vegas, decorated as Liberace's
life. Draw your own conclusions
about how much St. Dominic liked her song.
Saint Marina's father started her saint thing.
He so badly wanted the monk life: robes, &
silence, possible levitations, & dark navy
window morning songs, that he disguised Marina

as a boy and joined, bringing her/him along to
the monastery at Bithynia. Marina just kept in drag
even after her father bought the big one.
Even when she was accused of "fathering
the child of an innkeeper's daughter," she didn't
spill the beans. Instead, she silently took 5
years of expiation. Not until her death
was her innocence discovered. Let's all pray to Marina,
that great secret keeper, to help us keep our own freon
secrets from leaking toxic as PCB's, invisible,
& poisonous, & somehow necessarily satisfying.

What saves you from despair?
Who do you slam genuflect to?
Green Scapular with?
St. Lucy who carries 2 eyes in a dish?
Mary Magdalen & her ointment jar?
The winged-man Matthew?
The winged-ox symboled St. Luke?

An Oxygen Tent of Saints

Mulatto St. Martin De Porres is invoked
for interracial justice & harmony. St. Lawrence,
when the city prefect ordered him to hand over
all the valuables of the church,
assembled all the poor & sick; presenting them
to the prefect, he said, " 'Here is the church's
treasure.' . . . thereupon he was put to death
by being roasted on a gridiron."
St. Lawrence's emblem is a gridiron.

A Boarding House of Saints

St. Hubert, patron saint of hunters & trappers,
peppery, sacerdotal Hugh of Lincoln (emblem the swan),
Michael patron saint of grocers,
Martin De Porres patron saint of hairdressers,
Teresa of Avila patron saint of headache sufferers,

Paula patron saint of widows,
Anne patron saint of women in labor,
Clare of Assisi patron saint of television,
Benedict patron saint of speleologists,
Marculf patron saint of skin diseases,
Lidwina patron saint of skaters,
Gabriel patron saint of radio workers,
David patron saint of poets,
James patron saint of pilgrims,
Bernardine of Siena patron saint of public relations,
Antony the Abbot patron saint of grave diggers,
Michael patron saint of paratroopers,
Limping St. Ignatius of Loyola the heavenly patron of
spiritual exercises & retreats,
All the patron saints,
the levitating Joseph of Cupertino patron of airmen,
sweet, punctured Sebastian patron of archers,
Elizabeth of Hungary patron of bakers,

to all the burning angels & saints surrounding us, I
pray to your jigsaw spill bodies, your perfectly
preserved bodies. (Scrofulous St. Germaine of Pibrac
with her deformed right hand, St. Germaine who had
to sleep under the barn stairs & eat scraps, who left
her sheep to her guardian angel's protection
[she never lost one], St. Germaine who shared
her few scraps of food with beggars, St. Germaine
who was chased & beaten with a stick for "stealing
bread" to share, St. Germaine who when made to
unfold her winter apron only showed a fragrant
spill of summer flowers, St. Germaine died at 22.
Her dead body was found on her straw pallet
under the barn stairs. In death
St. Germaine's body lasted longer
than in life. 43 years after her death, her body was found
"in perfect preservation." 16 years later
"It was still flexible & well preserved." Then

she was put into the leaden coffin.)
Into the custody of saints I put my pop-rock bones,
my arsonist daylily soul. I ask the password
that saves, magnum opus? Viola da gamba? Kinnickinnic?

"Pray without ceasing" said that old misogynist St. Paul
and I confetti jog the saints' names through my bare soul.
Do Pow Wow, do Yom Kippur, do Bodi Day, Ta Chin, Shambala,
Christmas. St. Gregory the Enlightener suffered
12 torments. I'm on my way. I have to learn not to hang
mine out like wash, instead let them silently notch
my bones. To the pirate poet St. Godric,
after he walked barefoot across Europe
with his mother, the Virgin
Mary brought the Motown sound
and words of prayer.

We're in the Holy See.

Guy of Anderlecht prayed around:
seven years he shrine hopped.
(Brussel's cab drivers still do
an annual pilgrimage in his honor.)

Solitariness. Attentiveness.

That sunflower mystic Gertrude of Helftas
always did convent life, the always contemplative.
Her quest peaked in the big technicolor
Christ vision.

Unceasing interior prayer is the continual
striving of spirit toward God. Mother Theresa.

Marcellus the Righteous advocated manual work
and poverty. He was one of the "sleepless monks,"
one who sang Temptations' sweet
songs 24 hours a day.

". . . prayer itself will reveal to you
how it can become
unceasing."

Sunflowers, gladiolus. Snow.

St. Hildegard had 26 visions.

There are saints in night
clubs. There are saints with you
in desperate straits, doing the Hullabaloo,
doing lake prayers, awash in prayer
and saints. Eat stones.
Lake swim. Build of yourself.
Abandon force. Breathe. Again.

June 2, Saint Elmo's Day

The crows fly crazy consecrating electrical blue
shadows everywhere. The May Full Flower Moon
gone. The dominating June ghost rains here.
Magical as foxglove all June's renewable
pleasures. Tooled in me like a child's birth,
all the lovely returning
voices and shapes of birds and wind
and flowers; abandoned as saw music these
constant seasonal curious angel masses.
In the sacramentary month of June
there are lunatic flowers & ghost voices. Verbs
are what we try to put on time,
names of months on the filling,
or what falls from the sky,
colors the trees, colors.
All these controversies of grace.
There is such a thin layer of skin between each of us
& enormity. There is so little wood between
the outside and our ghost-forest sleeps.
We are saints with clubs following delicate
lost voices like seasonal roads you are
only allowed on sometimes. In
dominoes you choose from a boneyard.
In June your choices are unlimited.

Saint Aldhelm's Head

Saint Aldhelm (Bishop. b. in Wessex, c. 640;
d. at Doulting in Somerset, 709). Yep,
it goes that quickly. Do the math: 69 years.
But we're told "His brief episcopate was marked
by energy and enterprise." Unlike so many
suspicious women saints, for example: Felicity,
"martyr: birth date unknown, . . . put to death on the 23
of November in an unknown year, and buried
in the cemetery of Maximus on the Salarian Way.
Her story is lost," or St. Faith: "The accounts
of her passion are late and quite untrustworthy. . . .
the concatenation of names is itself suspicious,
and there is no good evidence that these martyrs
(another St. Faith, SS. Hope & Charity,
whose mother was Saint Wisdom) had any but a legend-
ary existence." You get the idea. Aldhelm
is the saint who was the first vaudevillian.
In public places, he mixed gospels and hymns
with jokes and tap dancing. "Did you hear the one . . . ?"
shuffle, shuffle. ". . . hoping thus to 'win
men's ears, and their souls.'" The main question
I have for Saint Aldhelm is this:
In his long Latin poem in praise of holy maidens
and a treatise on virginity (written for the nuns
of Barking in Essex), is he joking?
Or is he preaching?

"The cape in Dorset usually called St. Alban's Head
is properly titled St. Aldhelm's Head."

Saint Christina the Astonishing, 1224

"Nothing is more memorable than a smell,"
says Diane Ackerman, and I don't think she
even knows about Christina the Astonishing
who at the age of twenty-two, after
a particularly violent seizure, was thought
to be dead. During her Requiem Mass,
in fact right after the *Agnus Dei*,
Christina sat upright in her open coffin
then "soared to the beams of the roof,
and there perched herself." Her jet
propelled coffin exit emptied the church,
only her sister saw Christina's burial
Mass to its conclusion. After the Mass,
the priest made Christina come down. She
explained it was the smell of "sinful
human bodies" that catapulted her
to the roof. (I have heard repeated accounts
that people struck by lightning smell
like toast. What do those struck by grace,
by God, smell like? Coq au Vin?)
"We live in a constant simmering," says
Ackerman, "There is a furnace in our cells,
and when we breathe we pass the world
through our bodies, brew it lightly,
and turn it loose." Well,
Christina the Astonishing, who swore at 22
she actually had died, in fact had been to
hell, purgatory, and heaven, and met
friends in all three locales, hated
the simmering human potpourri.
For the rest of her life, and she lived
52 more years, Christina the Astonishing
tried to escape from the sinful smell of humans.
During prayers, she curled up like a bowling ball.
She fled to remote places: caves & towers,

& nunneries & the Count of Looz's castle all
to "escape the sinful smell of humans."
(Do sins smell sour-milk bad? Do serious
sinners smell worse than occasional sinners?
What is the worst smelling sin?)
Last summer, right before each flower
I had waited all through winter for
was to bloom, the rabbits ate the swollen
packed, almost colored blossoms. The rabbits
were fat with the color of flowers
that I never saw, but that they tasted.
A professional gardener told me to stuff
pieces of my old panty hose with my hair
and tack these little body shed ornaments
around the earth beneath my flowers.
She promised me the rabbits would disappear
hocus pocus fast. Are garden rabbits like Christina
the Astonishing? Are their fat, flower-fed bodies
repelled by the always sinful smelling
bodies and hair of people planting amazingly,
sinfully, colorful gardens all around them?

The Mongolian Contortionist with Pigeons

was breath taking, a flesh knot. There were
many fine Czechoslovakian skaters
that Olympic year. Each ended her act,
like a hyphen or parenthesis, lying
on the ice in dramatic, bad American music.
We watched the Olympian skaters Triple Axel
in heaven while L.A. burned a nervous breakdown.
In New Jersey runny eggs were outlawed, but
firearms were allowed, more threatening
than the teeth of an aye-aye. Locally
the smelt fishers didn't register a change:
up & down all night their parachute nets.
Lake Michigan smelled like arithmetic:
fog trees, fog trees, bluets. There were
grocery store epileptics and alphabet
annunciations, and constellations
of life's commonsensical commitments,
the human contracts: godmothers, godlovers,
godchildren, godhusbands. And you my
eye-rhyme, twin trick, sister fast
forwarded to death, dropped your skin body
inconsequentially as junk mail into
the planetary mailslot ragbag. You
left a note: The dog needs a walk, & 2
Emily Dickinson poems, peppered with granite
lips. The shepherd, Saint Cuthbert,
from his field, watched angels carry
the bishop, Saint Aidan, in a globe of fire
to heaven. The men who rolled you out of
your house in a Holy Communion white body
bag wore seethrough shower caps & rubber
gloves. The medical examiner was pregnant,
the priest fat. Oh how I head-talk to God
and my love dead. I have never lived 2 days
inside the same body. I have never 2 days

been married to the same man. In my garden,
the red bleeding heart bush made it through
our long winter. The white bleeding heart
didn't. On the blunt end of a heart's foreclosure,
you count flowers; you remember the landscapes
of you.

In the Relic Tent

In the sweet religiosity of snow:
the houses of the saints, the cloud forest,
St. Dympa, the transvestite saints,
Euphrosyne and Eugenia, the Redemptorists,
the hermits, the Desert Mothers, the apostates,
and nuns, the visionary Bernadette
and her Sisters of Charity at Nevers,
the warrior saints: Joan of Arc, Maxine
Hong Kingston, George & Procopius.
In our brief episcopates listen
to the mystagogic whispers of saints,
the privilege of poverty, the favor of dreams,
the beauty of holiness, & psalmody
& snow, the monastic habit & all
these holiness thangs: St. Clare
carrying the monstrance, blue birds
flying from the host, St. Columban driving
away the water monster from the river Ness
with only the sign of the cross; my mother
putting the saints' bones in my sleeping
bed; Cyriacus the Recluse never eating
before sundown and never being overcome
by anger. In the revival tent of saints
& poets, tremblers & shakers, the saints'
orchestra plays the romance factory sound
St. Cecily (emblem the organ) is wearing pink
tulle off the shoulder. She's playing
a 10,000 Maniacs' song, and, like always,
I'm a breath away from St. Vitus's dance,
like Berryman, like Wilbur, like Malcolm,
like Heather, like all the holy tremblers
I shake, like Sexton, often, I have to tie
myself in Turk's-head knots not to shake.
I tremble at all the holy beauty & terror
of the world: snow & mass murders,

prie-dieu & politicians. I have loved
the blue death hand & danced the dirty
dog with Twistin' Harvey; I have fasted
with the Poor Clares, watched in the fields
of Sextus as St. Cyprian stripped down
to his underwear for his beheading, watched
as the kid on Locust was stripped & killed
for his triple-down-filled coat.
With the suicide sisters I've read Demetrius
of Rostov's *Spiritual Alphabet.* I have had
my soul smashed like dalmatians, like TR4's,
like rich kids' MG's. For the truth
of the private museum of spiritual history,
I tell you this is no morbid religiosity.
This is redemption. This is true:
Age is this name-dropping confession.
Saints & poets never celebrate the day of birth,
dies natalis, they celebrate
the day of burial, the day of death.

The Heart's Dragnet

In the confraternity of nights'
lost cry dream signatures,
hot aluminum dreams flesh names
in the lake night sparklers. On bricks,
the eyes' arithmetic weather rumors
skin, bright, predatory skin takings.
Always the saint temptation: withdraw
from the world. Bread & hair shirts.
Saint Wulfric, summer & winter, nightly
would sit in a tub of cold
water until he had recited his whole
psalter. In my own angry hard love
unlearnings, under dissimilar clouds,
often bushwhacked, I learn how little I
can afford the world. I study
words' fugitive passageways, saints'
ration cards, & other sanctuaries
of invisibility. In the soul's always
dragnet, in the body's always priest,
in all periscope mornings I quest
my own body for its white holes,
its snow monkeys. In the soul's always
dragnet for the grace notes there are
nests of unseeking kindnesses: peglegs,
cookies, & Celtic lapidary ornamentations.
My dead mother using my daughter's voice
asks: "How, even now, can you
afford your life of poems?"
And in my own sanest moments I answer
them both back: "In this always
spinning fast disappearing
world, how can I not?"

In the Cellophane Rain

The cellophane souls we create in mirrors
instant a glitter feeling of fish
scales in the slideslip corner
of our eyes' leaves parachuting rosaries,
conducting through lightning everyday.
Every day is a day
someone someone has loved
has died on. My mother died
blue as irises. We
should not be afraid of colors;
just love every we are. Instants'
windfalls through a pedaling landscape.
Don't take a limousine; the limousine
takes what's best of us away.
Use the carp sidewalks. The lovely
carp sidewalks, exhilarating as sea horses,
ice glaze over fresh fallen leaves.
Blizzard's snow churches walk warm in
confused cathedrals. Set a boulder
as ballast, a boulder, alone on our altar
keeping our hearts from tilting west
with gewgaws. Read the zydeco saints,
chase what seems like nothing,
and love, always love in unimagined ways,
ways that anticipate dreams and snow.

The Cultus of Bones

Detonated bones, pepper
bones, tin morning
bones, monastery bones,
still in body bones,
fire bones, softened
with grace bones, boulder
colored draped with skin
parent bones, the scrap
bones, the pistachio colored
martyr bones, the never
pregnant pope bones, papacy
da da pontificate pop
song bones, modern
art black abstract bones,
baby dessert cloud bones,
ascetic pirate praying
bones, smuggled bones,
political bones, astrology
bones, aluminum bones,
the prophecy of bones. This is
the true transfer of relics: all
of us spinning to flowers & saints
in the pilgrimage of our death
happy dirt-fed bones.

God Sightings

Will you let me love everything?
What does your trampled body do
under your rough clothes
when violet Morrissey music plays?
Wearing my father's yard gloves,
I dance catalpa drunk in fluted
blossoms and red thrown
from heaven paisley mother kisses,
star eyeglasses, moon crutches, and
botanical playing cards. I'm a
walking genetic junk yard,
a tannery on a hot July
night: light, stink, and noise
from every yellow opened window.
I hate being crushed easily
as a concertina or a star gazing lily.
In this drunk gathering arsonist life,
what do you hide from the flames?
Why the always hurry to dismantle
every fragrant loud miracle?
A rabbit kickboxing a crow, a
tickertape rain clothespin holding
heaven to earth, reminding us of saints
and apples, and our puddle of earth
our jewel bones will rest in.
I have never seen all of God
only the red-glow tip of Her cigarette
on midnight porches and the raspberry
dipped birds, flying reminders like hula
hoops from Her sweet punctured body to mine.

I, the Excommunicate

A trinity, excommunicate, noun
verb and adjective. I am this
excommunicate doing the God pogo stick
in the blood relics. St. Januarius' glass
phialed blood, housed in the cathedral
at Naples, has liquefied and dried
18 times a year for 500 years.
I look like I'm playing God hooky, doing
the God jut, but I'm sitting in the God
furniture, feeling the rope burn of God.
St. Budoc's mother, Azenor, was thrown
in the sea off Brest in a cask "wherein
she gave birth to Budoc . . ." (My cousin
Kathy gave birth in a taxi cab.) Five
months later, Azenor & Budoc "were cast
up, alive and well on the coast of Ireland."
The kicker: the saint makers canonized
Budoc instead of his mother. I'm playing
the God games. God smells like melting
February, like the flowering miracle,
winter aprons of St. Elizabeth of Hungary,
St. Elizabeth of Portugal, St. Rose
of Virterbo, & St. Germaine of Pibrac.
I am driving the God car. I have put out
my God traps. I am putting out feeder lines
to God: prayer flags, prayer wheels, artichokes,
prayer beads, prayer birds, prayer songs, (do wha
ditty ditty dum ditty yea), prayer words.
Before my Holy Ghost bedtime, I, this completely
perishable excommunicate, am doing the big in-
timate grocery shopping with God; look
in our basket: State Fair corn dogs & tater tots.
And after shopping, we're going to do the big
snowy rec room slow dance. St. Joseph
of Copertino, the ecstatic, nicknamed

"the gaper," frequently levitated.
He was "excluded from much of the daily life
of his order because of the disturbance
caused by his raptures," and I'm shaking
the whole while I'm doing this freefalling
in the irregular wildernesses of God.